HEAT

FUNDAMENTALS

Other books in the FUNdamental Series
Light FUNdamentals
Electricity and Magnetism FUNdamentals
Mechanics FUNdamentals
Sound FUNdamentals

HEAT

FUNDAMENTALS

FUNtastic Science Activities for Kids

Robert W. Wood

Illustrated by Rick Brown

Chelsea House Publishers

Philadelphia

Library of Congress Cataloging-in-Publication Data

Wood, Robert W., 1933-
    Heat fundamentals : funtastic science activities for kids / Robert
W. Wood : illustrated by Steve Hoeft.
    x. cm. — (FUNdamentals)
Originally published: New York : Learning Triangle Press, c1997.
Includes index.
    ISBN 0-7910-4842-X (hardcover)
    1. Heat—Study and teaching—Activity programs—Juvenile literature.
I. Hoeft, Steve. II. Title. III. Series:
FUNdamentals (Philadelphia, Pa.)
QC256.W63 1997b
536'.078—dc21   97-28364
                                                                CIP

CONTENTS

INTRO

This book explores the fascinating world of heat. Although we take heat for granted, it's vital to all living things. *Heat* is the combined energy of all the moving molecules of something. *Molecules* are tiny particles that make up all materials, such as iron, glass, and wood. You can't see them or feel them, but these molecules are in constant motion.

We know that a body in motion has *kinetic energy*. The faster something moves, the more kinetic energy it has. And the more kinetic energy something has, the more heat it has, too.

Because all objects have moving molecules, they all contain heat. Even though cold water feels cool to the touch, we know that it is warmer than ice. But even ice contains heat. Ice forms in fresh water at 0°C, or 32°F. (This is warmer than the temperature of your freezer, which is about −13°C, or 8°F.) An object becomes colder when part of its heat is removed and the molecules are slowed down.

You don't need fancy equipment or complicated experiments to observe the behavior of heat. Though the activities in this book are easy to perform, they illustrate important principles about the world around us. Each activity begins with a challenge, followed by a materials list and

a step-by-step procedure. Results are given to explain what is being demonstrated, as well as a few questions to discuss further. The experiments conclude with fun facts.

Where measurements are used, they are given in both the English and metric systems as numbers that will make the activities easy to perform. Use whichever system you like, but realize that the numbers might not be exact equivalents.

Be sure to read Safety Stuff before you begin any experiment. It recommends safety precautions you should take. It also tells you whether you should have a teacher or another adult help you. Keep safety in mind, and you will have a fun-filled experience.

SAFETY STUFF

Science experiments can be fun and exciting, but safety should always be considered. Parents and teachers are encouraged to participate with their children and students.

 Look over the steps before beginning any experiment. You will notice that some steps are preceded by a caution symbol like the one next to this paragraph. This symbol means that you should use extra safety precautions or that the experiment requires adult supervision.

Materials or tools used in some experiments could be dangerous in young hands. Adult supervision is recommended whenever the caution symbol appears. Children need to be taught about the care and handling of sharp tools or combustible or toxic materials and how to protect surfaces. Also, extreme caution must be exercised around any open flame.

Use common sense and make safety the priority, and you will have a safe and fun experience!

Here's a chance to get in hot water—
and get away with it!

Heat Sink

Your Challenge

To discover the difference between heat and temperature.

Do This

1 Run some very warm water from the faucet. Fill both the cup and the bowl with water. (Figure 1-1)

Fill the cup and the bowl with water.

Make sure the water isn't hot enough to scald yourself!

Very warm tap water

Glass coffee cup

Large glass bowl

Thermometer

Figure 1-1

1

2 Place the thermometer in the cup and measure the temperature. (Figure 1-2)

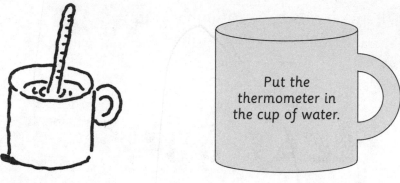

Put the thermometer in the cup of water.

Figure 1-2

3 Now measure the temperature of the water in the bowl. (Figure 1-3)

Put the thermometer in the bowl of water.

Figure 1-3

4 Compare the temperatures. What do you see?

WHAT HAPPENED?

Heat is a form of energy. It is the combined energy of all of the moving molecules of something. *Temperature* is simply the measure of the average energy of individual molecules of the object. Two objects can be at the same temperature, but if they are different sizes they will contain different amounts of heat.

Because the water came from the same source, both temperatures should have been about the same. Which container has the most heat? Can you think of a way you could use this information to design a method to store heat for later use?

If the molecules stopped moving and there was no heat in the object, the object would be at absolute zero. Absolute zero is equal to –273.15°C (–459.67°F).

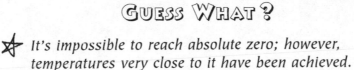

GUESS WHAT?

★ It's impossible to reach absolute zero; however, temperatures very close to it have been achieved.

★ *Cryogenics is the study of matter at extremely low temperatures. At these temperatures, air becomes a liquid and living tissues freeze instantly. At extremely low cryogenic temperatures, matter behaves even more strangely: liquids run uphill and electric currents flow forever!*

★ Heat energy occurs naturally within the earth and represents a potentially inexhaustible source of energy.

★ About 65 percent of the homes in Iceland are warmed by water heated inside the earth.

This is one hot experiment!

HOT HANDS

YOUR CHALLENGE

To use your sense of touch to detect temperature.

DO THIS

1 Align the bowls in a row and fill the first one about half full with very cold water.

2 Fill the middle bowl about half full with water at room temperature.

⚠ 3 Fill the one on the right about half full with very warm water. The water should be almost hot, but not hot enough to burn you.

4 Place your left hand in the cold water and your right hand in the very warm water. Leave them in the water a few seconds. (Figure 2-1)

YOU NEED

Three large bowls

Tap water (very warm, room temperature, and very cold)

> Put your left hand in the bowl of cold water and your right hand in the bowl of very warm water.

Figure 2-1

5   Now take your right hand from the very warm water and quickly place it in the middle bowl with the water at room temperature. What do you feel?

6   Remove your right hand and place your left hand from the cold water into the middle bowl. What do you feel now?

7   Place your left hand back into the cold water and your right hand back into the very warm water. Leave them there several seconds. Then quickly swap hands.

8   Place the hand from the cold water into the warm water and the one in the warm water into the bowl of cold water. Can you explain the differences in the temperatures you feel?

WHAT HAPPENED?

In each case, the temperature you felt should be much warmer or colder than the actual temperature of the water. Using your sense of touch can only give a relative measure of temperature, not an accurate one.

GUESS WHAT?

★ *When you shiver from the cold, it's the body's way of increasing heat production. (Figure 2-2)*

★ *Nearly all the energy from the food we eat leaves the body as heat.*

Brrrrrrrr!

Figure 2-2

This activity will tickle your tongue!

PEPPER RALLY

YOUR CHALLENGE

To demonstrate how heat can be created from any form of energy, such as electrical, chemical, and mechanical.

DO THIS

1 Turn on the lamp and hold your hand near the bulb. What do you feel? What kind of energy do you think this is? (Figure 3-1) (Hint: Is it plugged in?)

YOU NEED

Lamp

Hot pepper, such as a jalapeño

Bare hands

Place your hand near the lightbulb.

Figure 3-1

9

2 Touch the pepper to the tip of your tongue. What do you feel? What do you think causes this feeling? (Figure 3-2)

Touch the pepper to your tongue.

Try touching it to different parts of your tongue to see if it feels the same.

Figure 3-2

3 Briskly rub your hands together for a few seconds. What do you feel? Why do you think this happens? (Figure 3-3)

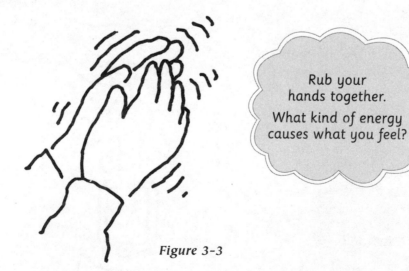

Rub your hands together.

What kind of energy causes what you feel?

Figure 3-3

WHAT HAPPENED?

One way to produce heat is through electrical energy. When an electrical current flows through a wire, such as the filament inside the lightbulb or the heating elements in a toaster, the wire puts up some resistance to the current. This resistance creates heat.

The pepper demonstrates how chemical energy can produce heat. Hot peppers, also known as chiles, contain a crystalline substance called *capsaicin* (cap-SAY-uh-sin) that gives them their hotness. Chemical action from the pepper produced heat in your tongue. The heat from a burning wood fire is also created from chemical energy; oxygen combines with burning wood, causing a chemical action that generates heat.

A third way to produce heat is by mechanical means. As you rub your hands together, friction between the two surfaces produces heat. Similarly, when you step on the brakes of a bicycle, mechanical energy from the brake pads rubbing against the wheel produces friction that generates heat.

Heat energy can also be changed into other forms of energy. For instance, heat energy from burning coal can be used to change water into steam, producing mechanical energy to drive turbines that, in turn, generate electrical energy.

> Did you use a jalapeño in the experiment?
> It measures 2,500 to 5,000 on the Scoville
> scale (see next page). Plenty hot!

GUESS WHAT?

★ A pepper's hotness is measured in Scoville units, or the number of units of water it takes to make a pepper lose all its heat. Very mild peppers, such as pimientos, are 0 Scoville units, while very hot peppers, such as Scotch bonnet and habañero varieties, can be as many as 150,000 to 300,000 Scoville units. Hot enough to cause severe burns to the skin!

★ Applying a car's brakes continuously for long periods, as when driving down a long hill, can generate enough heat to cause the wheels to emit a strong odor and even smoke. (Figure 3-4)

That dude should give his brakes a break!

Figure 3-4

It's time to twist and turn!

HOT WIRE

YOUR CHALLENGE

To observe how friction generates heat.

YOU NEED

Length of stiff wire about 12 inches (30 cm) long

DO THIS

1 Grasp the wire so that you can make a bend in the middle and begin bending the wire back and forth. (Figure 4-1)

Bend the wire back and forth. A thin coat hanger will work.

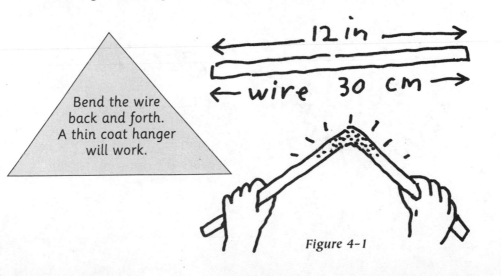

Figure 4-1

13

2   After about five or six times, feel the bend in the wire. What do you feel? Do you think the wire is weaker at this point?

WHAT HAPPENED?

When the wire is bent, the molecules in the metal are rubbed against each other. The friction of this rubbing generates the heat.

How do you think this principle would affect bridges made of steel? How would tall towers be affected by winds?

GUESS WHAT?

★ *All living things need heat, and the most important source of heat for us is the sun.*

★ *The surface temperature of the sun is about 5,500°C (10,000°F), which is too hot for normal flames to exist. (Figure 4-2)*

10,000°F

SUN

Because it's closer to the sun, the temperature on Venus is 459°C, or 858°F!

Figure 4-2

14

You'll have this one
nailed in no time

HAMMERED HEAT

YOUR CHALLENGE

To observe how pressure generates heat.

DO THIS

1   Feel the nail. It should feel cool to the touch.

2   Put on safety goggles and ask an adult to help. Place the nail on its side on the iron base and strike the pointed end several times with the hammer. The nail will begin to flatten. (Figure 5-1)

3   Feel the nail again. Now what do you feel? Do you think the nail is softer? If so, how would you make it harder? (Figure 5-2)

YOU NEED

Large nail

Safety goggles

Hammer

Heavy iron base (sledgehammer, vise, or anvil)

Figure 5-1

Figure 5-2

WHAT HAPPENED?

The moving hammer has kinetic energy. When the hammer hits the nail, this energy is transferred to the nail in the form of heat. Also, the nail begins to change shape. The molecules of the nail are forced to move the instant the hammer strikes. This transfer of energy and the rapid movement of the molecules generate heat.

GUESS WHAT?

☆ The temperature of the earth's core can reach about 4,500°C (8,100°F).

☆ Heat flows continuously from the core of the earth to the surface. (Figure 5-3)

☆ The temperature below the surface of the earth increases at a rate of about 5°F (3°C) for every 330 feet (100 meters) down.

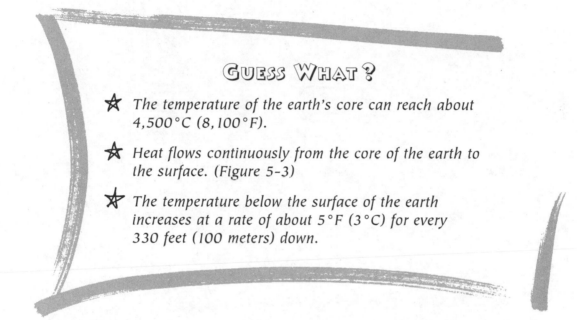

Earth's core

Heat flows

Figure 5-3

Heat flows out from the earth's core.

Did you know that scientists recently discovered the earth's inner core might spin faster than the surface?

That means every 400 years, the core makes an extra revolution!

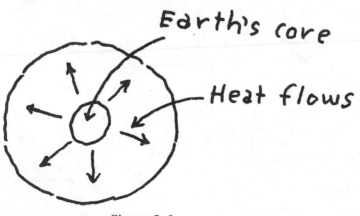

In this one, you'll see how molecules get around.

WAX FACTS

YOUR CHALLENGE

To observe how heat can change solids to fluids.

DO THIS

1   Warm the cup with the hair dryer, then place the ice cube in the cup. What do you see? Measure the temperature in the bottom of the cup. (Figure 6-1)

2   Place about 16 cubic cm (1 cubic inch) of paraffin in the aluminum pot. Place the end of the thermometer next to the paraffin.

⚠ 3   Heat the bottom of the pot with the hair dryer and monitor the temperature. What do you see? (Figure 6-2)

YOU NEED

Glass coffee cup

Hair dryer (handheld blow-dryer)

Ice cube

Thermometer

16 cubic cm (1 cubic inch) of paraffin (wax)

Small aluminum pot

Figure 6-1

Heat the cup with the hair dryer.

thermometer

wax

pot

Heat the bottom of the pot with the hair dryer.

Figure 6-2

20

What Happened?

When you add heat to a solid object, you speed up the movement of its molecules, which causes the solid to expand. If you add enough heat, the solid will change to a fluid, allowing its molecules to move more easily. This process is called *melting*. Heat caused the ice cube to change to a liquid at about 0°C (32°F), while the paraffin melted at about 52°C (125.6°F).

Why do you think high temperatures are necessary for welding or soldering?

Guess What?

✭ Lava flowing from a volcano can reach temperatures of 850° to 1,250°C (1,500 to 2,300°F).

✭ Lightning bolts are about the same size in diameter as a pencil but can generate temperatures reaching 28,000°C (50,000°F). (Figure 6-3)

✭ Lightning causes about 10,000 forest fires each year. In unpopulated areas, forest fires can be beneficial in regenerating forests. Beneficial fires clear underbrush and destroy the least healthy plants, leaving more moisture and nutrients for the trees.

Figure 6-3

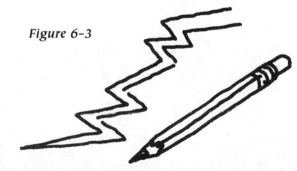

What a shocking fact!

21

Chill out!

FREEZE-OUT

YOUR CHALLENGE

To discover the freezing point of different fluids.

DO THIS

1   Fill the cup with about 2.5 cm (1 inch) of tap water, then place it in the freezer compartment of the refrigerator. Don't fill the cup up all the way! Leave it there for about an hour. (Figure 7-1)

Figure 7-1

Fill the cup with water.

23

2   Use the knife to shave off a small sliver of wax, and place it in the pot. Heat the bottom of the pot with the hair dryer. (Figure 7-2)

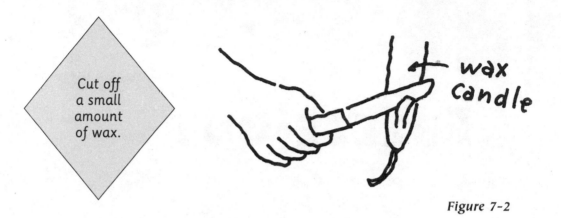

Cut off a small amount of wax.

wax candle

Figure 7-2

3   When the wax has melted, measure the temperature of the liquid. Then place the pot in the sink and run cold tap water around the bottom of the pot. What do you see? (Figure 7-3)

Figure 7-3

Run cold water around the pot.

4   Remove the cup from the freezer and examine the water. What do you see?

WHAT HAPPENED?

The temperature at which a liquid changes to a solid is called the *freezing point*. We know that the water changed to a solid at 0°C (32°F), and you observed that the wax changed to a solid at a much higher temperature. What do the results of your experiment tell you about freezing points? Are freezing points necessarily cold?

How would different freezing points affect the storage of foods, such as ice cream and butter?

GUESS WHAT?

★ Lead freezes at 327°C (620°F), and iron freezes at 1,535°C (2,795°F).

★ Some frogs can survive even when 65 percent of their body water has turned to ice. (Figure 7-4)

Frogs are called "cold blooded." This means a frog's internal body temperature changes based on its surroundings

Can you think of any other kinds of cold-blooded animals?

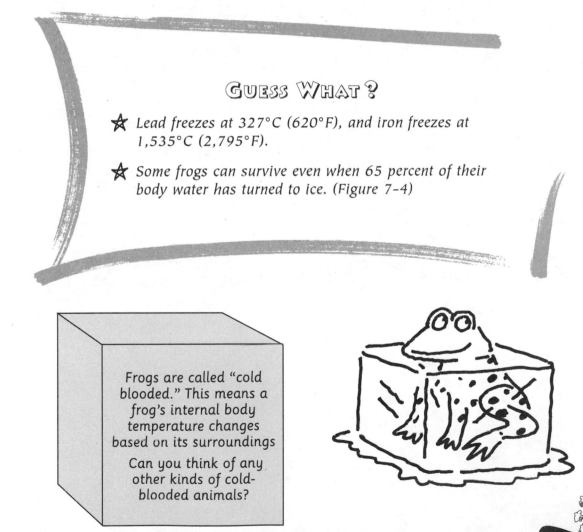

This one will have you steamed!

Gas Blast

Your Challenge

To observe a liquid changing into a gas, then back to a liquid.

Do This

1 Carefully fill the cup two-thirds full with hot tap water.

⚠ 2 Place the glass upside down on top of the cup and leave it a few seconds. (Figure 8-1)

3 Raise the glass a few inches, and watch the space between the cup and the glass. What do you see? What happens to the inside of the glass? (Figure 8-2)

You Need

Glass coffee cup

Hot tap water

Clear drinking glass, about the same size across as the cup

Place the glass over the cup of hot water.

Careful, you don't want this to be a shattering experience!

Figure 8-1

Lift the glass up a little.

Figure 8-2

28

WHAT HAPPENED?

Your glass acted like a "water heater." It heated the tap water to a point where the molecules were speeding around so fast that they formed a gas when exposed to room temperature. This gas could be seen as a smoky mist rising from the water. Because the glass was cooler than the gas, it caused the gas to *condense*, or change back to a liquid, and collect on the inside of the glass.

Can this help you explain how clouds form?

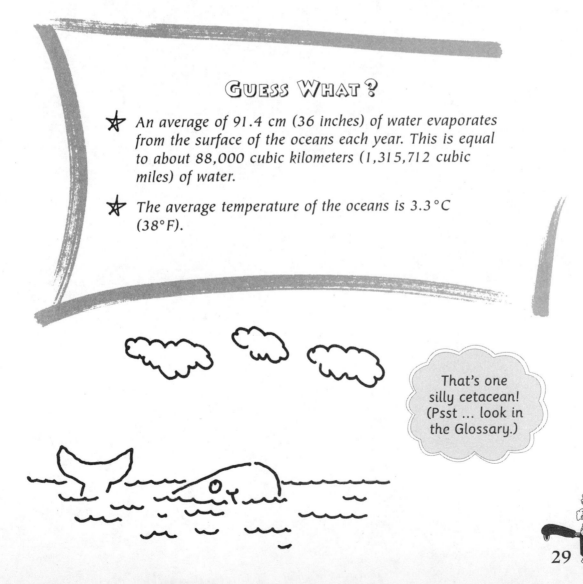

GUESS WHAT?

⭐ An average of 91.4 cm (36 inches) of water evaporates from the surface of the oceans each year. This is equal to about 88,000 cubic kilometers (1,315,712 cubic miles) of water.

⭐ The average temperature of the oceans is 3.3°C (38°F).

That's one silly cetacean! (Psst ... look in the Glossary.)

Butter your teacher up
by doing this one!

HEAT WAVE

YOUR CHALLENGE

To observe how different surfaces affect the transfer of heat.

DO THIS

1 Place the foil on a flat surface and use a pencil, ballpoint pen, or even your fingernail to make two circles about 1.3 cm (½ inch) apart. Make the circles about 4 cm (1½ inches) in diameter.

2 Mark an X in one of the circles. (Figure 9-1)

YOU NEED

Sheet of aluminum foil about 12 cm (5 inches) square

Black thick felt-tip marker

Margarine

Lamp with an incandescent (regular) lightbulb

Draw two circles and put an X in one.

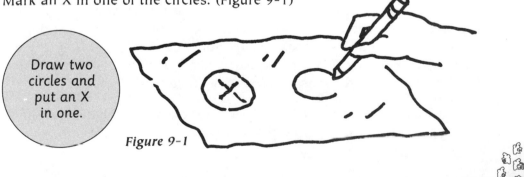

Figure 9-1

3   Use the marker to blacken the circle with the X in it.

4   Turn the foil over and blacken the other side of the *same circle*.

5   Place a small dab of margarine in each circle.

6   Remove any shade from the lamp and turn it on. Now hold the foil, margarine-side-up, over the bulb. Heat the area below the two circles. What do you see? (Figure 9-2)

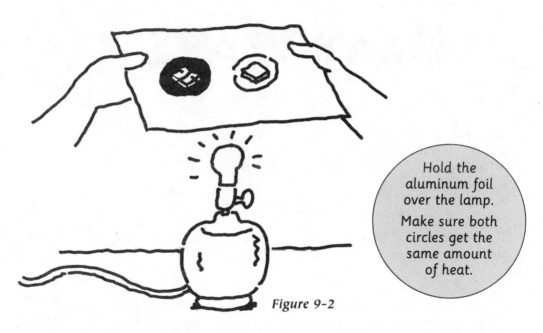

Hold the aluminum foil over the lamp.

Make sure both circles get the same amount of heat.

Figure 9-2

What Happened?

Heat from the bulb applied energy equally to the area below the dabs of margarine, but one of the circles became warmer. Heat energy, like light, is either absorbed or reflected, depending on the surface of the object being heated. Black surfaces absorb more heat energy. This is why on a clear summer day, dark surfaces such as a blacktop road can be much hotter than a nearby grassy area or a light colored sidewalk.

What color clothes would you expect to see worn in the desert? Should they be tight—or loose-fitting? Why?

GUESS WHAT ?

⭐ *Polished aluminum foil will reflect up to 95 percent of the heat striking its surface.*

⭐ *The highest natural temperature ever recorded was in the Libyan desert with a temperature of 57.8°C (136°F).*

That's a chic sheik!

Look out!
These molecules are on a collision course!

BUTTER FINGERS

YOUR CHALLENGE

To observe how heat moves
through an object.

DO THIS

⚠ 1 Use the nail to make three holes
     up the side of the can, or have an
     adult do it. The holes should be in
     a row and about 2.5 cm
     (1 inch) apart. (Figure 10-1)

> Hammer three
> holes along the side
> of the can.
>
> Make sure the can
> is anchored so it
> doesn't roll.

Figure 10-1

YOU NEED

**Empty aluminum
soda can**

Three toothpicks

**Nail a little larger
than the toothpicks**

Cold tap water

Margarine

**Lamp with an
incandescent
(regular) lightbulb**

35

2   Rinse the can with cold water to chill it. (Figure 10-2)

Rinse the can with cold water.

Your dad might say he's making chilly-can-corny!

Figure 10-2

3   Slide a toothpick about halfway into each hole, and pack it in place with a small mound of margarine.

4   Remove any shade from the lamp and turn it on.

5   Hold the can with the toothpicks sticking straight up, and place the bottom of the can against the side of the lightbulb. Hold it in this position for 2 or 3 minutes. What do you see? What happens to the toothpicks? (Figure 10-3)

Hold the bottom of the can against the side of the lightbulb.

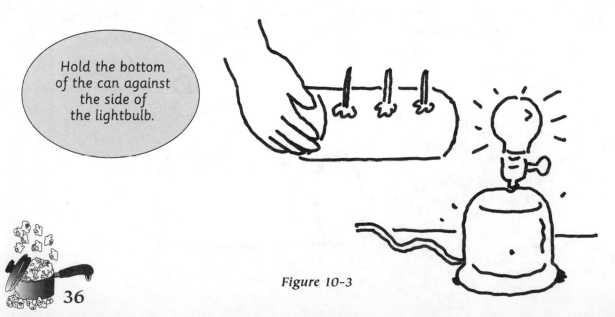

36

Figure 10-3

WHAT HAPPENED?

The molecules of the can near the bulb become hot, move more rapidly, and strike the cooler molecules next to them. These molecules, in turn, strike the molecules next to *them* and cause the adjoining molecules to move faster and get hotter. This will continue until the molecules at the other end of the can are reached. This transfer of heat energy through a solid is called *conduction*.

Which way does heat flow? Why?

GUESS WHAT?

⭐ When a spacecraft enters our atmosphere, tremendous heat builds up, not on the front of the vehicle but just ahead of it, because of the great compression of air. This superheated air becomes electrically charged, surrounds the spacecraft, and blocks all radio communications. (Figure 10-4)

⭐ Heat from the sun can cause exposed parts of a spacecraft to become very hot, while the shaded areas will cool below the freezing points of fluids such as water. Overall temperatures are controlled by rotating the spacecraft in a line with the sun. This motion is known as passive thermal control, *or the* "barbecue mode."

Figure 10-4

This is why, during the Apollo 13 spaceflight's re-entry, radio contact was lost and no one knew if the crew was okay at first.

Convection, vection...
what's your direction?

CONVECTION INSPECTION

YOUR CHALLENGE

To observe how heat changes the densities of parts of a fluid, causing the fluid to move in currents called *convection currents*.

DO THIS

1   Fill the coffeepot about two-thirds with cold tap water and set it aside. (Figure 11-1)

2   Fill each soda can with hot tap water, and place the cans together to form a base for the coffeepot.

3   Place the coffeepot on top of the cans, and allow it to sit about 10 minutes.

4   Put about three drops of food coloring in the water in the pot. (Figure 11-2)

YOU NEED

Glass coffeepot or beaker

Cold tap water

Four empty aluminum soda cans

Hot tap water

Food coloring

Sheet of white paper

You'll need a glass coffeepot and four aluminum soda cans.

Figure 11-1

Put three drops of food coloring in the water.

Use your favorite color!

Figure 11-2

40

5   Stand the white paper against the back of the coffeepot. From the near side, look through the cold water. What do you see? (Figure 11-3)

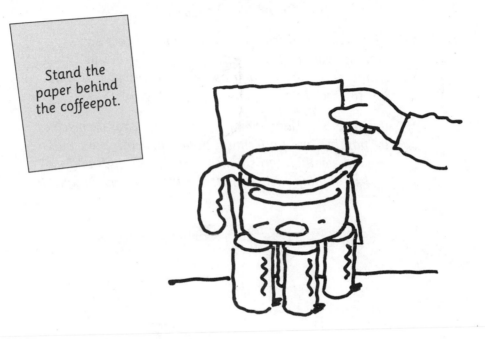

Stand the paper behind the coffeepot.

Figure 11-3

WHAT HAPPENED?

Heat causes fluids to expand and become less dense. Cooler fluids are more dense. Because of gravity, the cooler fluids sink and push the warmer fluids up toward the surface. This creates currents called *convection currents*. Heat can be transferred from one area to another by these currents. Air, which is a fluid, is often heated in one part of a room and travels to another area by this method.

Why is the upstairs of a house usually warmer than the downstairs?

GUESS WHAT?

⭐ *The heat generated by a person during one day's activity would be enough to raise his or her body temperature by as much as 149°C (300°F) if it were not for the water in body tissues. (Figure 11-4)*

⭐ *Because birds lack sweat glands, they cool themselves by panting and fluttering a pouch beneath their bills. In cold weather, birds conserve heat through body fat and by fluffing their feathers to increase insulation.*

Boy, that guy looks steamed!

Figure 11-4

Figure 11-5

You don't need to be
an airhead to do this one!

POURING AIR

YOUR CHALLENGE

To observe how cold, dense air affects our weather.

YOU NEED

Empty coffee can

Freezer

DO THIS

1 Place the coffee can in the freezer. Leave it for about 5 minutes.

2 Remove the can and hold out your hand, palm up.

3 Turn the can upside down over your palm. What do you feel? Is this air heavy? Why or why not? (Figure 12-1)

Turn the can upside down over your palm.

Careful, don't drop that air!

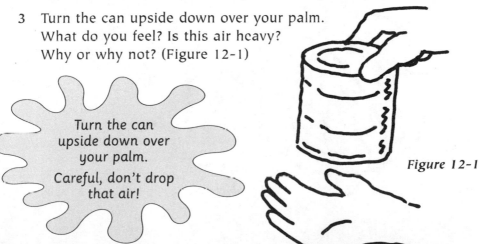

Figure 12-1

45

WHAT HAPPENED?

Heat causes fluids to expand and become less dense. Cooler fluids are more dense. Because of gravity, the cooler fluids sink and push the warmer fluids up toward the surface. This creates currents called *convection currents*. Heat can be transferred from one area to another by these currents. Air, which is a fluid, is often heated in one part of a room and travels to another area by this method.

Because heat from the sun is more concentrated at the equator, air is heated, becomes less dense, and moves farther up in our atmosphere. The poles receive much less heat from the sun, so these areas are much cooler. This cool polar air flows toward the equator to replace the warm air that went up. The warm air is cooled as it rises and flows toward the poles. At the poles, it sinks, replacing the air that moved toward the equator. (Figure 12-2)

When the warm air rises, it picks up moisture. But when the air cools, the moisture condenses and falls as rain. Weather patterns are formed by these currents of air.

Warm air rises; cold air sinks.

Figure 12-2

GUESS WHAT?

⭐ *The windiest place on earth is along the southern coast of Antarctica, with gale winds of 320 kilometers (200 miles) per hour.*

⭐ *The coldest naturally occurring temperature ever recorded was in Antarctica at -89.2°C (-128.6°F). (Figure 12-3)*

Figure 12-3

48

Check out this rad
radiation experiment!

RAY DISPLAY

YOUR CHALLENGE

To observe how heat and light travel through space in rays.
The energy is called *radiant energy*. The process is called
radiation.

DO THIS

1   With the lamp off, hold your hand, palm up, 5 to 8 cm
    (2 to 3 inches) from the bulb. What do you feel?

2   Turn on the lamp. Now what do you feel? (Figure 13-1)

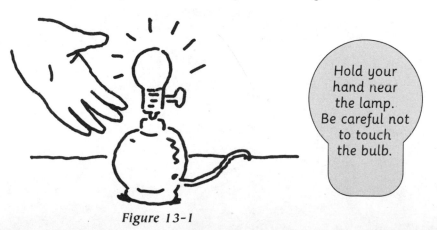

Hold your
hand near
the lamp.
Be careful not
to touch
the bulb.

Figure 13-1

WHAT HAPPENED?

Heat travels by radiation almost instantly. When heat travels by radiation, it can even travel across a vacuum, which is a space that is empty of matter. Heat from the sun warms the earth by radiation across the vacuum in space.

How could this type of energy be used to heat water or a house? How could it be used to produce electricity in rural areas?

GUESS WHAT?

★ *The earth's crust is broken up into plates 70 to 150 kilometers (40 to 90 miles) thick that float on a mixture of molten rock and gases called* magma. *At 400 to 700 kilometers (250 to 430 miles), temperatures may be greater than 1,100°C (2,000°F). The plates shift at about the same rate that your fingernails grow, about 1.3 to 5 cm (.5 to 2 inches) a year. (Figure 13-2)*

★ *Groundwater trickling down on the hot rocks above the magma is heated to temperatures as high as 205 to 260°C (400 to 500°F). Where openings occur, the heated water will rise to the surface as hot springs. (Figure 13-3)*

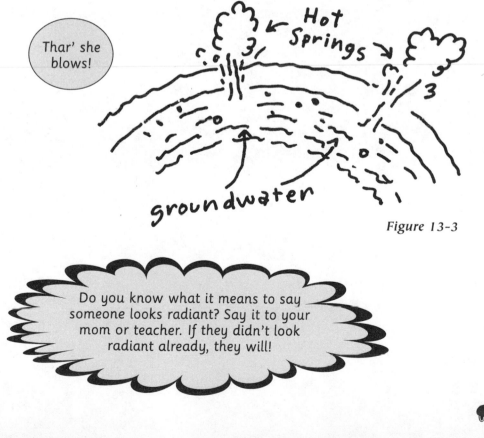

Figure 13-2

Magma is hot, liquefied rock deep below the earth's surface. When magma rises to the earth's surface through cracks or volcanoes, it's called lava.

Thar' she blows!

Figure 13-3

Do you know what it means to say someone looks radiant? Say it to your mom or teacher. If they didn't look radiant already, they will!

Ever had your head in the clouds?
You will with this experiment!

VAPOR CAPER

YOUR CHALLENGE

To observe how heat changes saltwater into rainwater.

DO THIS

1 Tear off a sheet of plastic wrap large enough to completely cover the larger bowl and set it aside.

2 Pour about 2 cm (¾ inch) of hot tap water into the larger bowl.

3 Add 3 tablespoons of salt and a couple of drops of food coloring. Stir the solution. (Figure 14-1)

Plastic food wrap

Glass bowl about 15 cm (6 inches) in diameter

Hot tap water

3 tablespoons salt

Food coloring

Spoon

Small glass bowl about 7.5 cm (3 inches) in diameter

Rubber band (to go around larger bowl)

Weight, such as a small pebble or a coin

Ice cubes (2-4)

Put the salt and a couple of drops of food coloring in the water.

Figure 14-1

4   Place the smaller bowl in the center of the larger bowl.

5   Cover the top of the larger bowl with the plastic wrap, but allow the plastic to sag about 5 cm (2 inches) in the center. Place the rubber band around the bowl to hold the plastic in place.

6   Place the weight on the plastic at a position over the small bowl. Place two to four ice cubes on top of the weight. Wait about 2 hours. What do you see? (Figure 14-2)

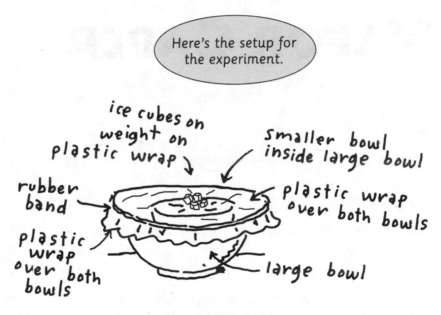

Figure 14-2

7   Remove the plastic wrap and examine the contents of the small bowl. What do you find? What color is it? Touch a little of the solution to the tip of your tongue. What does it taste like? Can you think of an emergency where this could be helpful?

WHAT HAPPENED?

Radiated heat from the sun makes water evaporate from the oceans, lakes, and rivers. This moisture-laden warm air rises until it mixes with cooler air. Because cold air cannot hold as much moisture, the moisture condenses into water droplets and forms clouds. The water droplets collect on tiny dust particles in the air. When the droplets become heavy enough, they fall as rain.

When water vapor cools and condenses into pure water, the process is called *distillation*. Saltwater from the oceans is distilled by the sun and turned into rain.

GUESS WHAT?

⭐ *Although there are several ways to remove salt from seawater, distillation is the most widely used process. The first land-based distillation plant was built in Kuwait nearly 50 years ago. Today, there are over 1,500 plants around the world.*

⭐ *About half of the world's distilled water is produced in the Middle East. (Figure 14-3)*

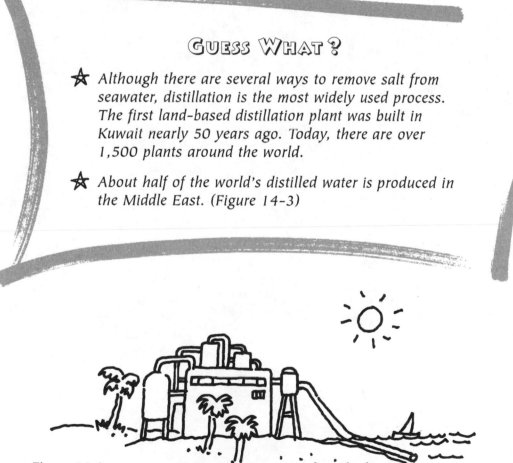

Figure 14-3

Can you guess why there are so many distillation plants in this part of the world?

Here's a hint: Think about the kind of weather in the Middle East and where it stands geographically.

You'll expand your ideas about heat with this one.

HOT-AIR BALLOON

YOUR CHALLENGE

To observe how heat causes air to expand.

DO THIS

1 Place the bottle in the freezer, or put it in a bowl and cover it with ice. Let stand about 5 minutes.

2 Remove the bottle and stretch the balloon over the top of the bottle. Place the bottle in the sink and run warm tap water over it. What happens to the balloon? Why do you think it happened? (Figure 15-1)

YOU NEED

2-liter plastic soda bottle

Freezer or large bowl of ice cubes

Balloon

Warm tap water

Sink

Run warm water over the bottle.

balloon →

2-liter soda bottle

Figure 15-1

WHAT HAPPENED?

When air is heated, the molecules of air move faster and farther apart. This causes the air to take up more space.

GUESS WHAT?

⭐ In 1987, British businessman Richard Branson and Swede Per Lindstrand were the first to fly a hot-air balloon across the Atlantic. The trip began at Sugarloaf Mountain, Maine, and ended 33 hours later in Northern Ireland. (Figure 15-2)

⭐ Extremely high-altitude balloons are used by scientists to study cosmic rays and gamma rays from outer space.

Are we there yet?

Figure 15-2

58

You'll get a rise out of this one!

MAGIC NEEDLE

YOUR CHALLENGE

To observe how heat causes objects to expand.

DO THIS

1 Thoroughly rinse the can with water to remove any residual soda.

⚠ 2 With the hammer, very carefully tap the needle into the bottom of the can, or have an adult do it. (The needle is made of steel and is much harder than the aluminum, so this shouldn't damage the needle.) The needle should be driven into the can just until it comes to the flattened part with the eye. You want a perfectly round hole that will allow the needle to slide in easily without falling through. (Figure 16-1)

YOU NEED

Aluminum soda can

Sink to rinse can

Small hammer

Sewing needle

Freezer

Sink

59

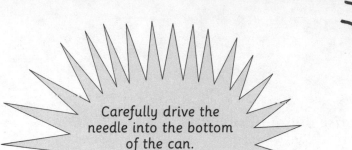

Carefully drive the needle into the bottom of the can.

Ask an adult to help you with this part!

Figure 16-1

3 Remove the needle.

4 Place the can in the freezer for about 10 minutes.

5 Remove the can from the freezer and place it upside down on a flat surface. Stand the needle in the hole.

6 Place your hands around the can and warm it. Watch the needle. (Figure 16-2)

Figure 16-2

Warm the can with your hands.

What happens to the needle?

60

What Happened?

Most substances expand when heated. The molecules of the substance move faster, spread apart, and occupy more space. This is why some sidewalks and concrete driveways are laid in sections, with gaps between each section.

Which bridge expands more in the summer, a long one or a short one? Why?

Guess What?

★ Some burglar alarms operate on the fact that all people and all objects give off heat. If an intruder enters the protected area, the increase in temperature sets off the alarm.

★ Infrared cameras are used in forest fires to detect any fires hidden by smoke. (Figure 16-3)

Figure 16-3

Can you guess how infrared cameras can also be used in smoke-filled buildings to save lives?

Did you know you can slow molecules down? Here's how!

CONTRACTION ACTION

YOUR CHALLENGE

To observe how air shrinks when cooled.

DO THIS

1   Blow up the balloon to a diameter of about 15 cm
    (6 inches), using the tape measure to check the diameter.
    Tie the opening of the balloon securely. (Figure 17-1)

Blow up the balloon.
You might need an
adult to knot the end.

YOU NEED

Small balloon

Tape measure

Two drinking glasses

**Tap water
(hot and cold)**

Sink

Figure 17-1

63

⚠ 2   Carefully heat both glasses by holding them under hot running water. Remove the glasses from the hot water and turn on a stream of cold water.

3   Quickly place the openings of the heated glasses to each side of the balloon and cool them under the faucet. What do you see? Can you hold one glass upside down and lift the other glass? (Figure 17-2)

Figure 17-2

Hold the balloon at the sides with the two glasses and run cool water over them.

What happens to the balloon?

WHAT HAPPENED?

The molecules of warm air move around rapidly and take up a certain amount of space. When the air is cooled, the molecules move more slowly and require less space.

GUESS WHAT?

★ High-temperature water, as high as 205° to 260°C (400° to 500°F) can erupt from chambers in the earth in the form of geysers.

★ Steamboat Geyser in Yellowstone National Park is the largest active geyser in the world. It once spewed hot water to heights of 150 meters (500 feet) for almost 15 minutes and gushed steam for about 40 hours. (Figure 17-3)

Did you know that Yellowstone National Park has over 3,000 geysers and hotsprings?

Figure 17-3

65

66

Do you carry a thermos in your lunchbox?
This activity will show
you how it works!

TRAPPING HEAT

YOUR CHALLENGE

To discover how some
materials can be used
to hold heat.

DO THIS

⚠ 1 Carefully use the
hammer and nail to
make a hole in the top of
each lid large enough to insert
the thermometer, or have an
adult do it. (Figure 18-1)

Carefully hammer a nail
into the top of each lid.

Be sure to take the lids off the
jars before you do this and rest
the lids on a surface you
can't damage!

Figure 18-1

YOU NEED

Hammer

**Nail, thicker than
thermometer**

**Two jars about the
same size, with lids**

Warm tap water

Thermometer

Modeling clay

Towel

Rubber band

67

2   Fill each jar about half full with warm tap water, then screw on the lids.

3   Insert the thermometer through the hole and measure the temperature of the water in each jar. Both readings should be about the same. (Figure 18-2)

Measure the temperature of the water in each jar.

Figure 18-2

4   Remove the thermometer and cover the holes with clay. (Figure 18-3)

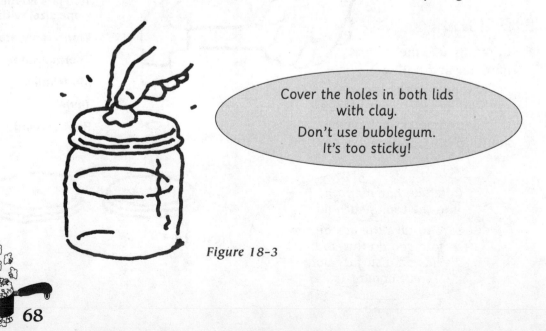

Cover the holes in both lids with clay.

Don't use bubblegum. It's too sticky!

Figure 18-3

5   Wrap one of the jars with a towel and fasten it in place with the rubber band. (Figure 18-4)

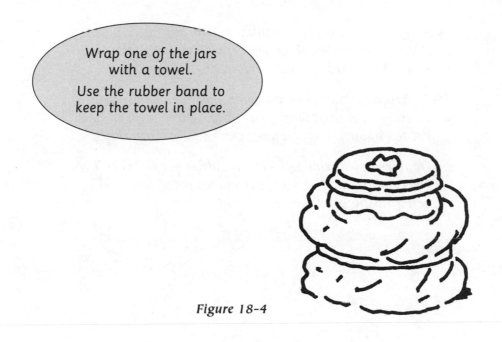

Wrap one of the jars with a towel.

Use the rubber band to keep the towel in place.

Figure 18-4

6   Measure the temperature of the water every couple of minutes and record the results. What do you observe after monitoring the temperatures for several minutes?

WHAT HAPPENED?

When something is heated, the molecules pass heat on to the neighboring molecules, losing a little heat in the process. Heat always tries to move toward something colder. Air is a good insulator, so anything that traps air, such as the towel, will tend to prevent the transfer of heat.

How do thermos bottles work? If something holds heat in, can it also be used to hold in cold? Why or why not?

GUESS WHAT?

⭐ Still air is an excellent insulator. Two centimeters (¾ inch) of enclosed airspace insulates better than 10 cm (4 inches) of solid concrete.

⭐ Superinsulation, made of mylar, has been developed recently. It is used mostly in space, where protection is needed against temperatures close to absolute zero.

⭐ Double-paned windows have an air space between two pieces of glass. The air space makes these windows better insulators than glass alone.

You'll make a really cool
thermometer in this experiment!

THERMOMETER FACTORY

YOUR CHALLENGE

To observe how a thermometer works.

DO THIS

1   Drop a few drops of food coloring in the bottle, and fill the
    bottle to the top with cold tap water.

2   Mold the clay around the straw about 12 cm (5 inches)
    from one end of the straw. This will be the top of the
    thermometer. Do not cover the end of the straw.

3   Place the other end of the straw down into
    the bottle, and mold the clay around
    the bottle opening so that no
    air can escape. (Figure 19-1)

Place the straw down in
the bottle and mold the clay
around the bottle opening.

Make sure there aren't any
air pockets.

Figure 19-1

YOU NEED

Glass bottle (pint, quart, or liter size)

Food coloring

Cold tap water

Modeling clay

Clear drinking straw

Bowl or pot of warm water

Cooking oil

Ruler

Pencil or ballpoint pen

White card about 7.5 x 12.5 cm (3 x 5 Inches)

Transparent tape or thread

71

4   Place the bottle in the pot of warm water for about 5 minutes. What do you see?

5   Remove the bottle. Now what happens?

6   Add a drop of cooking oil to the water in the straw to keep the water from evaporating.

7   Use the ruler to mark off a scale on the card. Make the marks at 1-cm (.5-inch) intervals. Number the marks from 1 to 10. Although your readings will not be in Fahrenheit or Celsius degrees, your thermometer will indicate a rise and fall of the temperature.

8   Using clear tape or thread, carefully attach the card to the back of the straw. (Figure 19-2)

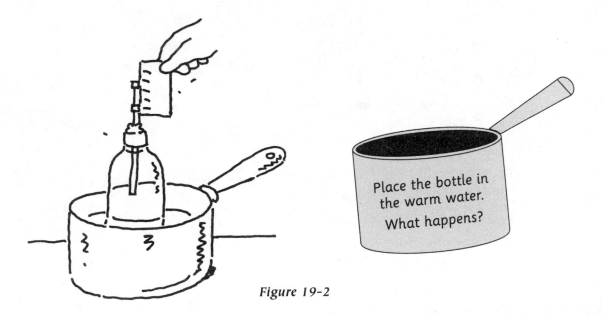

Figure 19-2

9   Take your thermometer outside and record the readings at different times of the day. What do you observe? Can you record temperatures below freezing? Why or why not?

> Do you know what liquid is used in
> most regular thermometers?
>
> Here's a clue: Which planet is
> closest to the sun?

WHAT HAPPENED?

Water, like most fluids, expands when heated and contracts when cooled.
(However, water is unique because, when it cools enough to freeze, it
then expands as ice.)

GUESS WHAT?

⭐ Ice skaters really don't skate on ice, but on a thin film
of water created by the pressure of the skates against
the surface of the ice. (Figure 19-3)

⭐ Freshwater freezes at 0°C (32°F), but seawater freezes
at about −2°C (28°F).

73

Figure 19-3

Bet you breeze right through this one!

COOL BREEZE

YOUR CHALLENGE

To observe the cooling effect of evaporation.

DO THIS

1 Wet your hand with water, then place it in the stream of air from a fan or blow on it. What do you feel? (Figure 20-1)

Place your wet hand in front of the fan.

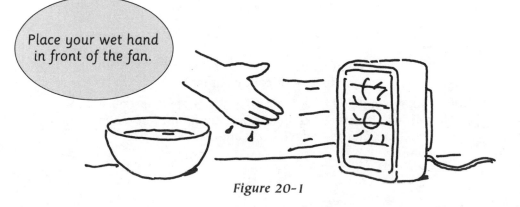

Figure 20-1

2 Make sure your hand is thoroughly dry. Now wet your hand with the rubbing alcohol and try it again. What do you feel this time? (Figure 20-2)

Figure 20-2

Try it again after wetting your hand with rubbing alcohol.
Be careful not to get any alcohol in your eyes!

WHAT HAPPENED?

The heat from your hand is removed from the surface of the skin as the water or alcohol evaporates. This lowers the temperature of the skin. Both water and alcohol cool, but because alcohol evaporates much faster, it cools more. The faster something evaporates, the more it dissipates, or lessens, heat.

How could this method of cooling be used for a building? Would it be useful in deserts? Why or why not? Would it be useful in the tropics? Why or why not?

Do you know why you can see your breath in cold weather?
Have you ever noticed how your breath is cool when you hold your lips closely together like you're whistling, but hot when you open your mouth wider? Try it and see for yourself!

GUESS WHAT?

★ *Radiators on cars are sealed to allow them to operate as much as 15 pounds per square inch over atmospheric pressure. This pressure raises the boiling point of the coolant to as high as 126.6°C (260°F).*

★ *If the cap on a hot radiator is suddenly removed, the boiling point of the coolant drops instantly, and the radiator boils over. (Figure 20-3)*

That car just needs to let off a little steam!

Figure 20-3

78

It's a heat race! And the winner is...

MARGARINE MELTDOWN

YOUR CHALLENGE

To observe how well different materials conduct heat.

DO THIS

1 Fill the glass with about 7.5 cm (3 inches) of hot water.

2 Place a small dab of margarine near the top of each item to be tested: the pencil and two spoons. Make the dabs the same size and at the same distance from the bottom of each item. For example, if one of the items is taller, place the dabs so that they will all be at the same height when the items are placed in the glass.

3 Stand the items in the glass. Use the towel to prop up the items and to cover the opening so that heat doesn't escape. Monitor the dabs of margarine for several minutes. What do you see? (Figure 21-1)

YOU NEED

Drinking glass or cup

Hot tap water

Margarine, grease, or butter

Wooden pencil

Metal spoon

Plastic spoon

Hand towel or small cloth

79

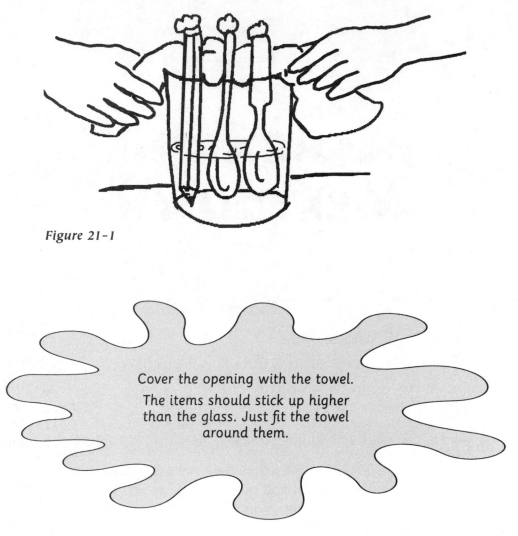

Figure 21-1

Cover the opening with the towel. The items should stick up higher than the glass. Just fit the towel around them.

WHAT HAPPENED?

Heat from the water travels toward the cooler parts of the test items, but different materials conduct heat at different rates. Which material is the best conductor? Which is the poorest?

Would the color of the test items make a difference? Why or why not?

GUESS WHAT?

⭐ Fires are classified according to the material that is burning. Class A fires involve ordinary combustibles such as paper, wood, and cloth; Class B fires cover flammable and combustible liquids, greases, and similar materials; Class C fires are those involving electrical equipment; and Class D fires are limited to combustible metals such as magnesium. (Figure 21-2)

⭐ Glass in windows, bottles, and mirrors is formed at temperatures of about 700°C (1,290°F).

Fire extinguishers are coded the same way fires are classified, but some kinds can be used for several different types of fires.

Check the extinguisher in your classroom to see what type it is.

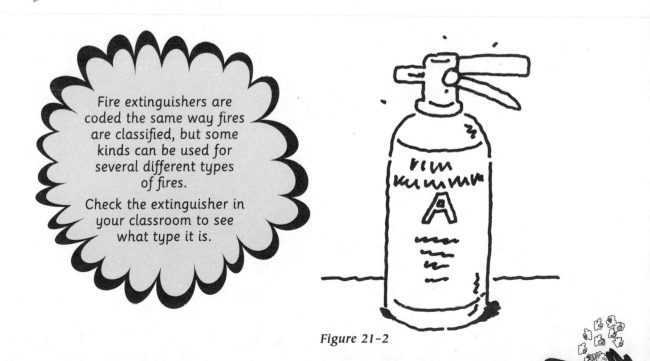

Figure 21-2

81

Did you know that copper can breathe?
Read on!

COOLING COPPER

YOUR CHALLENGE

To observe the expansion and contraction of copper.

DO THIS

1   Place the copper tube in the freezer while you gather the other materials.

2   Cut a strip of thin cardboard about .75 cm (¼ inch) wide and about 24 cm (9 inches) long for a pointer.

⚠ 3   Press the needle through the center of the cardboard strip and fasten it in place with tape or glue.

4   Place the copper tube lengthwise near the edge of a table. Clamp one end securely to the table, or use the weight to hold it in place.

YOU NEED

Length of 1.3-cm (½-inch) copper tubing about 60 cm (24 inches) long

Freezer

Scissors

Thin cardboard

Sewing needle

Tape or glue

Table

Clamp or heavy weight such as a brick

Hair dryer (handheld blow-dryer)

5 Place the needle under the tube about 5 cm (2 inches) from the other end. The end of the needle should extend past the edge of the table so that the pointer extends out as well. Turn the needle so that the pointer is pointing straight up.

6 Turn the hair dryer on *HIGH*, and blow hot air through the tube from the clamped end. Aim the hair dryer so that the air does not hit the pointer. What do you see? (Figure 22-1)

Blow hot air through the tube.
Make sure not to blow air on the pointer.

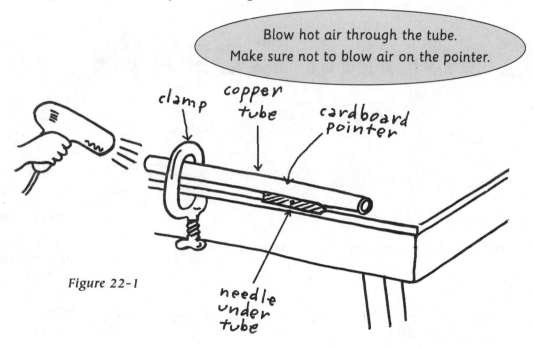

Figure 22-1

7 Turn the dryer on *COOL*. Now what happens? (Figure 22-2)

Blow cool air through the tube.

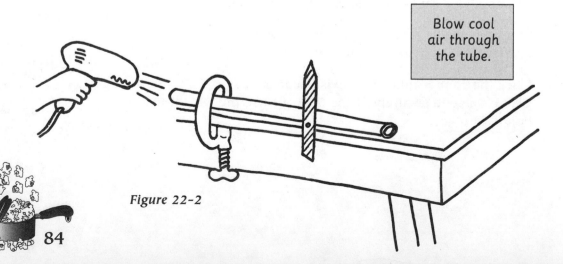

Figure 22-2

84

WHAT HAPPENED?

The hot air warms the tube, causing it to expand. Cool air makes the copper contract. This expansion rate is indicated by the pointer.

How would this expansion and contraction affect wires suspended from telephone poles in the summer? In the winter?

GUESS WHAT?

★ *A city's compact mass of buildings and pavement can alter the weather. A city generates heat and moisture because of its traffic, industries, and the heating and cooling of homes. It also produces a large amount of contaminants from its daily activities. The result causes a decrease in solar radiation, visibility, and horizontal wind speed, as well as an increase in air temperature, fog, cloudiness, rainfall, snowfall, and the number of thunderstorms. (Figure 22-3)*

★ *The engines on most cars, boats, and lawn mowers are heat engines. A heat engine converts heat energy into mechanical energy. If it were not for the cooling systems in engines, many of the parts would melt.*

Figure 22-3

Did you know that the word smog is a blend of SMoke and fOG?

This one will give you
that warm, fuzzy feeling!

WRAP SESSION

YOUR CHALLENGE

To determine whether blankets produce heat.

DO THIS

1 Notice the reading of the thermometer, then wrap it in the
blanket. Leave it in the blanket a few minutes, then check
the reading again. What do you see? (Figure 23-1)

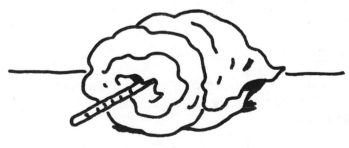

Figure 23-1

Wrap the
thermometer in a
blanket and check
the temperature.

2 Now wrap the thermometer and yourself in the blanket. Stay wrapped for a few minutes. Compare the reading. Now what do you see? (Figure 23-2)

Now wrap yourself in the blanket and check the temperature.

Figure 23-2

WHAT HAPPENED?

The blanket did not produce any heat, which is why the temperature didn't change in step 1. The blanket only helped contain the heat that was produced by your body.

GUESS WHAT?

⭐ When animals hibernate, temperature controls in their brains allow their body temperatures to drop to just above freezing. A hibernating animal becomes unconscious and is completely inactive. It is able to survive for long periods on the fat stored in its body. (Figure 23-3)

⭐ Scientists are studying hibernation to learn how it might be applied to humans. It could be useful for certain medical and surgical conditions and for prolonged travel through space.

Now that's an unaware bear!

Figure 23-3

Tell an adult that you might need to go
to the beach to do this one!

A DAY AT THE BEACH

YOUR CHALLENGE

To investigate the effect that heat has near bodies of water.

DO THIS

1 Place one thermometer in the jar of water, and insert the
   other one into the jar of dirt. (Figure 24-1)

YOU NEED

Two thermometers

Large jar of water

Large jar of dirt

Put one
thermometer in
the jar of water
and the other in
the jar of dirt.

Would this work
with sand? Try it
and see!

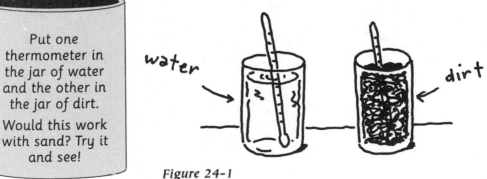

Figure 24-1

91

2 Place both jars in sunlight and monitor the temperatures over the next several hours. What do you see? How would a forest or a plowed field affect air movement?

WHAT HAPPENED?

Near the beach during the day, the ground warms the air, causing it to rise, and the cooler air from the sea comes in to replace it. At night, the ground is cooler than the seawater, so the air over the water rises and the air over the ground flows out. (Figure 24-2)

A seagull in sunglasses?
That's silly!

Figure 24-2

GUESS WHAT?

★ *Rising warm air in thunderstorms can create updrafts greater than 10 meters (33 feet) per second.* Microburst, *the outflow from intense downdrafts, can produce surface wind speeds over 290 kilometers (180 miles) per hour.*

★ *Ocean currents, like our atmosphere, are caused by the rise and fall of waters at different temperatures. It is thought that currents might even rise from the depths like smoke curling up from a fire.*

*Cleanup is easy—just eat
the evidence!*

POPPER PUZZLE

YOUR CHALLENGE

To investigate what makes popcorn pop.

DO THIS

⚠ 1 Have an adult heat some popcorn until it pops. Save a few unpopped kernels to look at later.

2 Listen for the noise that occurs. What do you hear? Why don't the kernels all pop at the same time? (Figure 25-1)

3 Eat the popcorn!

WHAT HAPPENED?

Each kernel of corn contains moisture. This moisture is contained in a hard, airtight shell. The heat causes this moisture to expand, creating pressure and causing the shell to burst. (Figure 25-2)

YOU NEED

Microwave oven or popcorn popper

Popcorn

Listen to the popcorn as it cooks.

Figure 25-1

Examine the popcorn kernels you saved.

Figure 25-2

GUESS WHAT?

⭐ A substance can burst into flame all by itself. This process is called spontaneous combustion, or self-ignition, and is caused when particles of the substance unite with oxygen. To prevent spontaneous combustion from occurring, coal is usually stored in shallow piles to dissipate heat.

⭐ Moist hay stored in a barn can generate enough heat to burst into flames. Spontaneous combustion can also be a safety hazard around the home. Rags saturated with oil, furniture polish, or paint can burst into flames if stored improperly. (Figure 25-3)

It's a bovine fire-buster!

Figure 25-3

Don't feel pressured into doing this one!

MELTING POINT

YOUR CHALLENGE

To observe how pressure affects ice.

DO THIS

1 Place the two ice cubes on a paper towel so that they are touching each other. After a few seconds, see if they are stuck together. (Figure 26-1)

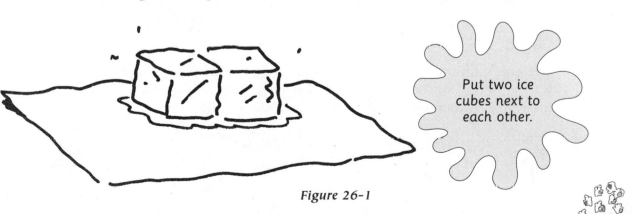

Figure 26-1

YOU NEED

Two ice cubes

Paper towel

Put two ice cubes next to each other.

99

2 Place one cube on top of the other and press hard. Both surfaces should be flat together. (Figure 26-2)

Press down on the top ice cube.

Figure 26-2

3 Release the pressure. Now what do you see?

What Happened?

The pressure lowered the melting point of the ice, and a small layer of water formed between the cubes. Then when you released the pressure, the water froze again and the cubes were stuck.

What happens when you walk on ice? Why?

GUESS WHAT?

⭐ *If all of the ice in Greenland and Antarctica melted today, sea level would rise nearly 65 meters (215 feet).*

⭐ *The ice cream you buy was frozen hard in rooms with temperatures of –23° to –28°C (–10° to –20°F).*

⭐ *The United States produces and consumes more ice cream than any other country.*

102

Do it right, and the ice will be twice as nice!

ICE SPLICE

YOUR CHALLENGE

To use pressure to cut an ice cube in half.

DO THIS

1   With string or tape, securely fasten the handle of the fork to the top part of the handle of the pot. The points of the fork should be level and pointing away from the pot. Mount the fork so that its prongs will form a cradle for the ice cube.

2   Now fill the pot with tap water and place it next to the sink so that the fork extends over the sink. The water is for weight to keep the pot from tipping.

3   Bend the tab of the soda can up to make a lifting point, and fill the can with cool tap water.

4   Feed one end of the wire through the opening in the tab of the can. Form a loop about 12 cm (5 inches) long and tie the wire in a knot.

YOU NEED

Fork

String or tape

Pot of water

Kitchen sink

Empty soda can

Thin copper wire about 30 cm (12 inches) long

Ice cube

Two small pieces of aluminum foil

5 Lift the can of water by the loop and hang the loop on the center prongs of the fork.

6 Place the ice cube through the loop so that it rests on the fork and so that the wire hangs over the top of the ice cube. Place a piece of aluminum foil between the ice and the fork on each side of the wire loop. This will slow the melting of the ice. (Figure 27-1)

Here's the setup for the experiment.

Figure 27-1

7 Now lower the wire so that the weight of the can is suspended by the ice cube. Monitor the ice cube for several minutes. What do you see? What happens to the can after 20 or 30 minutes? What happens to the ice cube? Why?

What Happened?

Gravity pulling on the can of water causes the wire to apply pressure on the ice. This pressure lowered the melting point of the ice, which melted and allowed the wire to move through the ice. After the wire moved, the pressure above the wire was gone and the melted ice refroze, sealing the opening. Because it was a copper wire, it also conducted heat from the air in the room.

Guess What?

⭐ *At arctic temperatures, steel and rubber become brittle.*

⭐ *Regular lubricants such as oils and grease cannot be used at arctic temperatures because they freeze.*
(Figure 27-2)

Hope that guy has a good battery in his car!

Figure 27-2

106

Don't be a wet blanket!
This one's fun!

WET BLANKET

YOUR CHALLENGE

To discover the heat protection of wet and dry cloths.

DO THIS

1 Wet one of the cloths with cool tap water and set it aside.

2 Fill the soda can with hot tap water.

3 Wrap the wet cloth around the can and cup your hands around the cloth. What do you feel? (Figure 28-1)

Wet cloth

Cool tap water

Empty aluminum soda can

Hot tap water

Dry cloth

Figure 28-1

Wrap the can with a wet cloth.

What do you feel?

4 Remove the wet cloth and wrap the dry one around the can. Cup your hands around the dry cloth. Now what do you feel?

What Happened?

Both cloths are made up of fibers with many insulating airspaces. Air is not a good conductor of heat. If the cloth is wet, these airspaces are lined with water, which is a much better conductor of heat. If you were to pick up a hot pan with a wet cloth or pot holder, the heat can turn the water into steam, which can travel through the wet fabric and burn your hand. Always be sure to use dry materials when handling anything hot.

Guess What?

 Elephants use their ears for air-conditioning. Warm blood from their bodies circulates through their fan-shaped ears, where it is cooled and returned to their bodies. (Figure 28-2)

★ Lowering the pressure lowers the boiling point. This means that on top of a high mountain, the atmospheric pressure lowers the boiling point of water to such an extent that the water cannot get hot enough to cook eggs satisfactorily.

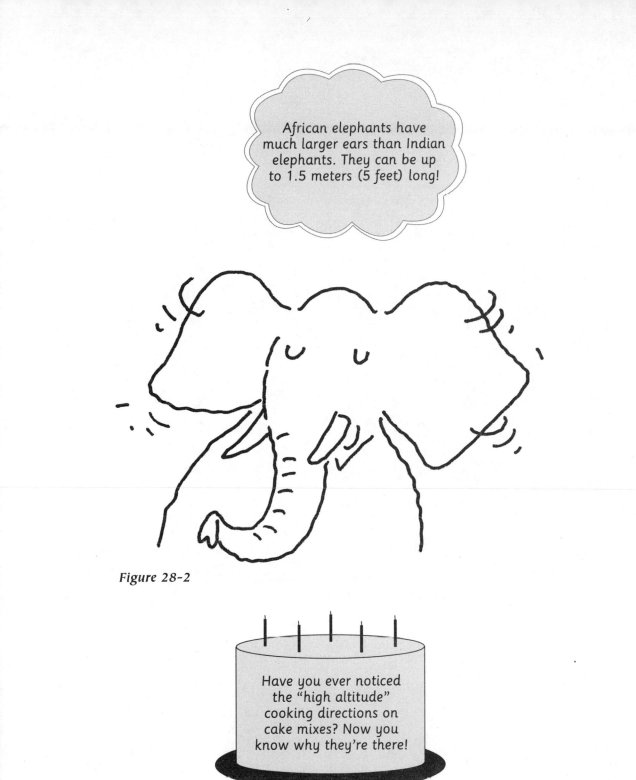

Figure 28-2

Pump it up!

INFLATION OBSERVATION

YOUR CHALLENGE

To observe the heat generated by compressed air.

DO THIS

1   Inflate the tire (or other object) with the pump. (Figure 29-1)

Inflate the tire with the pump.

Not too much. You don't want it to blow up!

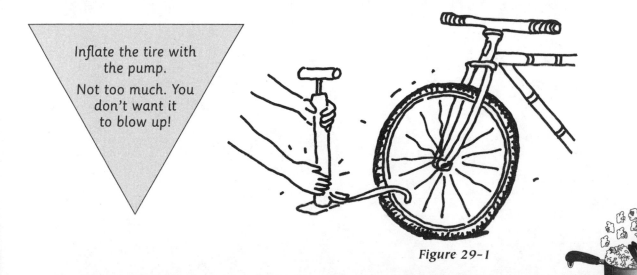

Figure 29-1

2   After several minutes of hard pumping, touch the lower part of the barrel of the pump. What do you feel?

WHAT HAPPENED?

Heat can be produced by friction. The bottom part of the pump is heated because the molecules making up the air are pressed closer together, and they are forced to rub against and strike each other more than normal. This rubbing and striking of the molecules is what produces the heat. Some added heat is also caused by the friction of the piston rubbing against the inside of the barrel.

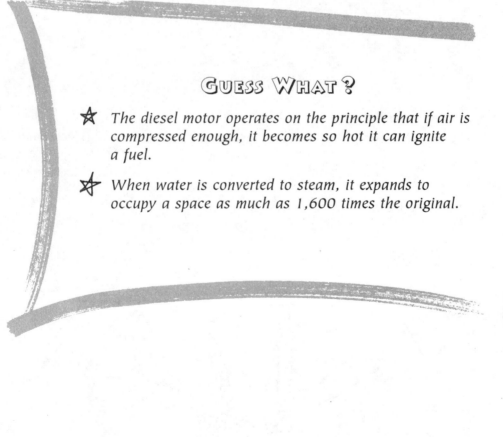

GUESS WHAT?

★   *The diesel motor operates on the principle that if air is compressed enough, it becomes so hot it can ignite a fuel.*

★   *When water is converted to steam, it expands to occupy a space as much as 1,600 times the original.*

This one'll have you spinning.

DIZZY DEVICE

YOUR CHALLENGE

To use rising currents of air to operate a device.

DO THIS

1   Cut the paper into a coil, or spiral. Make the turns about 2.5 cm (1 inch) wide. Be sure the center is wide enough to partially insert the thimble.

2   Make a hole in the center of the coil and press the bottom of the thimble partway through the hole.

3   Insert the needle upside down into the pencil's eraser so that the eye-end goes in first.

4   Remove the threaded nut, or finial, from the top of the lampshade, and place the spool over the threaded stud on the lamp.

5   Place the pointed end of the pencil into the hole in the spool. Carefully set the thimble in the spiral over the point of the needle. (Figure 30-1)

6   Turn on the lamp. What do you observe? Could this be used for power? Why or why not?

YOU NEED

Sheet of paper about 22 x 28 cm (8.5 x 11 inches)

Scissors

Metal thimble

Sewing needle

Wooden pencil with eraser

Empty thread spool

Table lamp with screw-on shade

113

Here's the complete setup.

paper coil

thimble

needle

pencil

spool

lamp

What Happened?

The point of the needle makes very little contact with the thimble, and this makes a very good pivot point with little friction. As the lamp begins to heat the air, the warmer air becomes less dense than the cooler air surrounding it, and the warm air begins to rise.

Guess What?

★ Heat cannot be seen or heard.

★ Hang-gliding pilots can work the updrafts along cliffs and fly long distances. The world's record for hang gliding is 303.4 kilometers (188.2 miles).

GLOSSARY

absolute zero The lowest *theoretically* possible temperature. Equal to
−273.15°C or −459.67°F. Although scientists have not been able to reach
absolute zero because they are unable to reduce gas any further than its
liquid form, they have come close.

boiling point The temperature at which a liquid boils. Water at sea
level boils at 100°C or 212°F.

Celsius A temperature scale where 0° is the freezing point and 100° is
the boiling point of water.

centigrade The old name for the Celsius temperature scale. It was
called the centigrade scale because the range between the freezing and
boiling points of water was divided into 100 degrees ("centi" comes from
a Latin word for hundred).

cetacean Pronounced si-TAY-shun. An aquatic sea mammal with a
torpedo-shaped, hairless body, two nostrils, and a horizontally flattened
tail used to move through the water. Examples include the whale,
dolphin, and porpoise.

condensation The process of reducing matter to a denser form, such as
vapor or steam.

conduction The movement of heat energy through a material.

convection The movement of fluids or gases caused by the different densities of the parts of the fluids: warm air rising and cold air falling, for example.

cosmic rays Streams of high-energy charged particles from outer space.

cryogenics The science that deals with the production of very low temperatures and their effect on matter.

density The ratio of the mass of something to it's volume. Density describes how compact something is.

distillation The process of first heating a mixture and then cooling and condensing the resulting vapor to produce a nearly pure or refined substance.

Fahrenheit The temperature scale where water freezes at 32° and boils at 212°.

freezing point The temperature at which a liquid freezes or becomes a solid. The freezing point of water is 0°C (32°F). This may also be the melting point.

gamma rays A stream or rays of electromagnetic radiation.

heat The transfer of energy from one substance to another, measurable by *temperature*.

infrared Invisible radiation generated by heat.

ionized To change or be changed into electrically charged atoms.

kinetic energy The energy of a body that results from its motion.

magma Liquid or molten rock deep inside the earth.

melting point The temperature at which a solid changes to a liquid. May also be the freezing point.

microburst A quick, violent downdraft of air that causes wind shears. Usually associated with thunderstorms.

molecules The smallest particle of a substance consisting of one or more atoms.

passive thermal control An action such as rotating a spacecraft in flight to avoid one area getting too much heat from the sun. Also called the "barbecue mode" because it resembles the action of roasting something on a spit.

radiation The process in which energy travels through space in the form of rays of heat, light, X-rays, etc.

spontaneous combustion The process of catching fire as a result of heat generated by internal chemical action.

temperature The measure of the relative hotness or coldness of something. Temperature can be distinguished from *heat* in that it is a property of a body, whereas heat is energy flow from a body.

INDEX

ABOUT THE GUY WHO WROTE THIS BOOK

A keen observer of nature and an avid follower of scientific advances, author Robert W. Wood injects his own special brand of fun into children's physics. His *Physics for Kids* series has been through 13 printings, and he has written more than a dozen other science books. His innovative work has been featured in major newspapers and magazines.